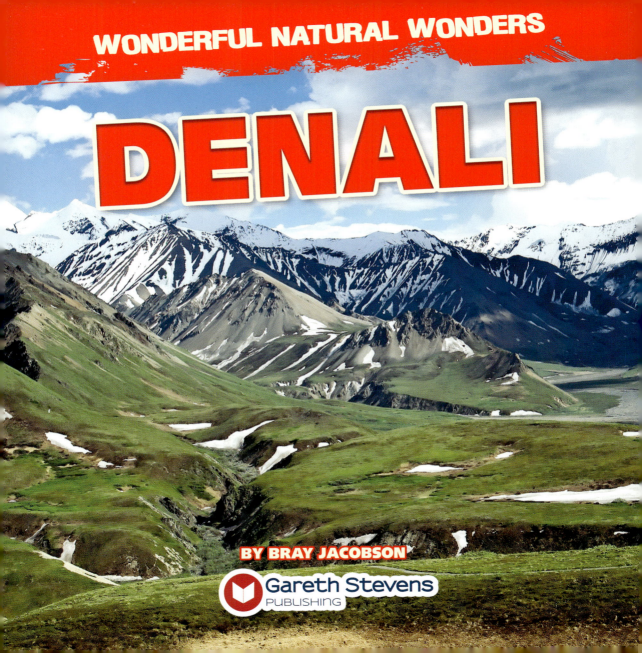

Please visit our website, www.garethstevens.com. For a free color catalog of all our high-quality books, call toll free 1-800-542-2595 or fax 1-877-542-2596.

Library of Congress Cataloging-in-Publication Data

Names: Jacobson, Bray, author.
Title: Denali / Bray Jacobson.
Description: New York : Gareth Stevens Publishing, 2023. | Series: Wonderful natural wonders | Includes index.
Identifiers: LCCN 2021036683 (print) | LCCN 2021036684 (ebook) | ISBN 9781538276709 (set) | ISBN 9781538276716 (library binding) | ISBN 9781538276693 (paperback) | ISBN 9781538276723 (ebook)
Subjects: LCSH: Denali National Park and Preserve (Alaska)–Juvenile literature. | Denali, Mount (Alaska)–Juvenile literature.
Classification: LCC F912.M23 J34 2023 (print) | LCC F912.M23 (ebook) | DDC 979.8/3–dc23
LC record available at https://lccn.loc.gov/2021036683
LC ebook record available at https://lccn.loc.gov/2021036684

Published in 2023 by
Gareth Stevens Publishing
29 E. 21st Street
New York, NY 10010

Copyright © 2023 Gareth Stevens Publishing

Designer: Tanya Dellaccio
Editor: Kristen Nelson

Photo credits: Cover Michael G McKinne/Shutterstock.com; background texture (pp 3-24) BEMPhoto_31/Shutterstock.com; p. 5 Lukas Bischoff Photograph/Shutterstock.com; pp. 7, 13 (background) arigato/Shutterstock.com; p. 7 (map) Ad_hominem/Shutterstock.com; p. 9 Uwe Bergwitz/Shutterstock.com; p. 11 Everett Collection/Shutterstock.com; p. 13 (top) MM_photos/Shutterstock.com; p. 13 (bottom) Roberto Lusso/Shutterstock.com; p. 15 Jay Yuan/Shutterstock.com; p. 17 Sherri Cassel/Shutterstock.com; p. 19 https://upload.wikimedia.org/wikipedia/commons/9/96/Denali_NP_map_NPS.jpg; p. 21 Matt McCullough/Shutterstock.com.

All rights reserved. No part of this book may be reproduced in any form without permission in writing from the publisher, except by a reviewer.

Printed in the United States of America

CPSIA compliance information: Batch #CSGS23: For further information contact Gareth Stevens, New York, New York at 1-800-542-2595.

CONTENTS

The Tall One 4
Where Is Denali? 6
Exploring Denali 8
Naming a Mountain 10
Freezing Cold. 16
In the Park 18
Climbing Denali. 20
Glossary. 22
For More Information. 23
Index 24

Boldface words appear in the glossary.

The Tall One

Denali is the tallest mountain on the North American **continent**. Its peak, or top, is 20,310 feet (6,190 m) above sea level. Known for centuries to the **native** peoples of Alaska, this natural wonder has been drawing explorers to Alaska since the 1700s.

Where Is Denali?

Denali is in Alaska. Alaska is northwest of most of the United States. It shares a **border** with Canada. Denali is south of the center of Alaska. It's north of the city of Anchorage, Alaska, and northwest of Alaska's capital, Juneau.

Exploring Denali

Denali was first written about by a non-native Alaskan in 1794. Russian explorers made maps that showed the mountain and area around it. By the time the United States bought Alaska from Russia in 1867, the huge mountain was well known.

Naming a Mountain

The name Denali comes from the native Koyukon Athabascan people. In their language, it means "the high one." Other native groups had names for the mountain too. Then, in the 1890s, a newspaper called it Mount McKinley after President William McKinley.

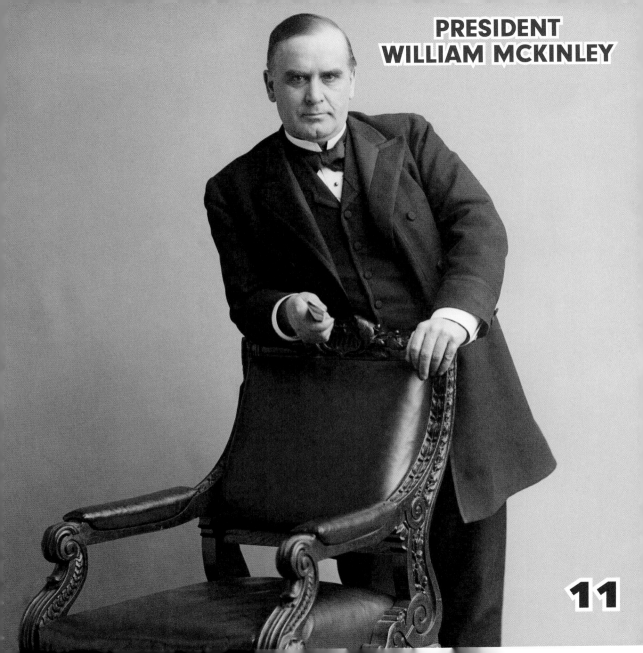

Many people didn't like this name. They believed a name used by a native group should be used. However, the U.S. government ignored these **protesters**. When a national park was created around the mountain in 1917, it was called Mount McKinley National Park.

U.S. POSTAGE STAMPS SHOWING MOUNT MCKINLEY

13

The state of Alaska officially called the mountain Denali in 1975. But it wasn't until 2015 that the U.S. government changed the mountain's name. Today, the park around the tallest mountain in North America is called Denali National Park and **Preserve**.

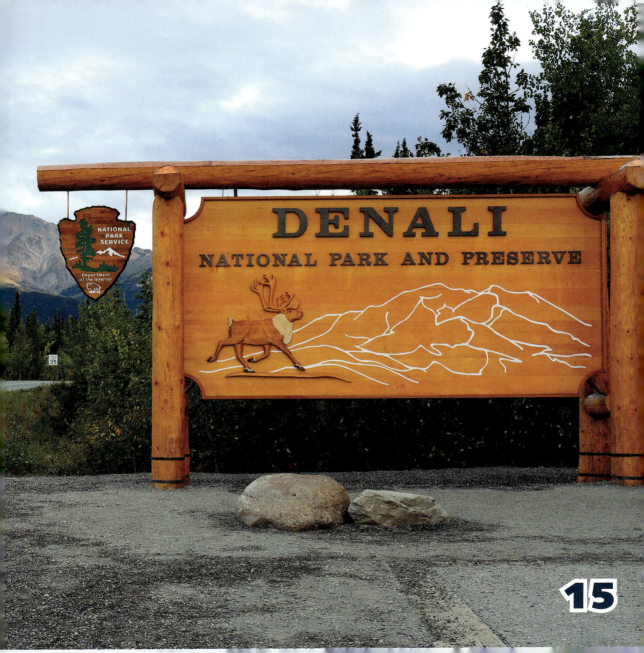

Freezing Cold

Denali's top half is always covered in snow and ice. It's so cold, there are even **glaciers**! It can be -75°F (-60°C) on the mountain. That's too cold for people and animals to live there.

In the Park

Denali National Park and Preserve is made up of 6 million acres (24,281 sq km) of land in Alaska. It includes the Alaska Range. There is one road running through the park. It runs from east to west and is 92 miles (148 km) long.

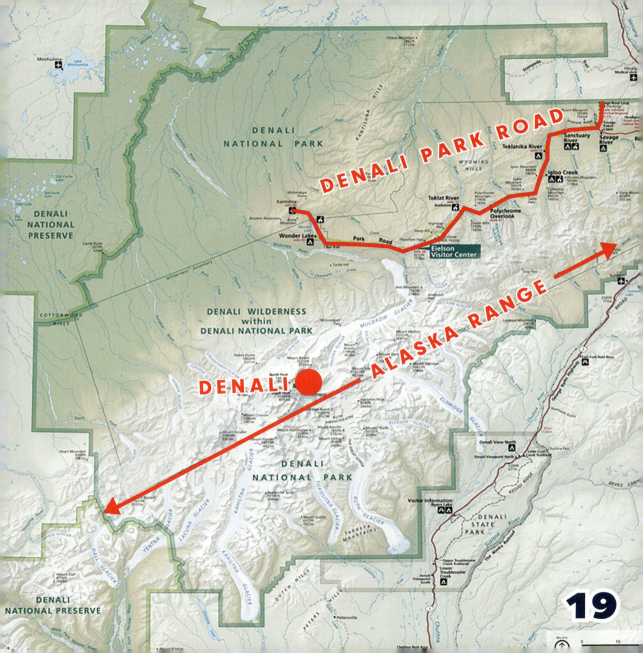

Climbing Denali

The first group to reach the south **summit** of Denali did so in 1913. Partly because of the cold, the mountain is **dangerous** to climb. Still, hundreds of people try to reach the summit each year.

GLOSSARY

border: a line separating one country or state from another

continent: one of Earth's seven great landmasses

dangerous: unsafe

glacier: a huge sheet of slowing-moving ice

native: having to do with a group of people who were living in an area, such as North America, when a new group of often European people arrived

preserve: a place set aside for animals and plants

protester: one who protests, or strongly opposes something

summit: the top of a mountain

FOR MORE INFORMATION

BOOKS

Daly, Ruth. *Denali*. New York, NY: AV2 by Weigl, 2020.

McHugh, Erin., et al. *National Parks: A Kid's Guide to America's Parks, Monuments, and Landmarks*. New York, NY: Black Dog & Leventhal Publishers, 2019.

WEBSITES

Denali National Park and Preserve
kids.nationalgeographic.com/nature/article/denali
See pictures and read about Denali National Park.

Denali National Park and Preserve
www.nps.gov/dena/index.htm
Find out more about visiting Denali National Park on the National Park Service's website.

Publisher's note to educators and parents: Our editors have carefully reviewed these websites to ensure that they are suitable for students. Many websites change frequently, however, and we cannot guarantee that a site's future contents will continue to meet our high standards of quality and educational value. Be advised that students should be closely supervised whenever they access the internet.

INDEX

Alaska 4, 6, 14, 18

Anchorage, Alaska 6

Canada 6

climate 16, 20

height 4

Juneau, Alaska 6

McKinley, William 10

national park 12, 14, 18

North America 4, 14

Russia 8

United States 6, 8